OCTOBER TIDES

Chris Ogborne

To Jane & Alan

With best wishes
Chris

Published in 2020 by Chris Ogborne

© Chris Ogborne 2020

ISBN: 978-1-5272-7009-1

Printed and bound in Great Britain by
Short Run Press Ltd, Exeter, Devon

*Dedicated to Edna, my mother
and my inspiration*

Preface

Who among us has stood at the sea's shore and, wondering at the vast horizon, not felt the urge to travel? The seas and oceans have always instilled in man a feeling of unrest and the need to discover new and exciting places. "I must go down to the seas again, to the lonely sea and the sky ..." wrote John Masefield.

Poets and writers through the ages have found ample ways of portraying their feelings about the sea. The young boy Thomas John Stone, my uncle, feels the pull of such a horizon and his local playground is a small Welsh beach – the sea his dream. With a zest for life, a twinkle in his eye, he keeps his eight siblings amused through the daily life and some hard setbacks which befall his family. Tom, with his elder brother and sisters, are free to roam and play in the streets of their South Wales town in the 1920's and run to the small local beach beside the tidal estuary making it their favourite playground. Skimming stones as far out to sea as he can and watching the ships passing in the distance, Tom fosters a growing desire to join the Royal Navy and see the world – a world which changes dramatically when the second world war begins and he is already based in Hong Kong.

From his happy childhood home in Wales, through his strenuous training regime in South Devon, Tom is living for both himself and his twin, who died in infancy, as he signs up for twelve years in the Navy aged eighteen. He succeeds as a fully trained Leading Stoker based at HMS Tamar in Hong Kong and serves on HMS Thracian at a particularly tense time in 1940. As the war increasingly involves the Far East, the fall of Hong Kong on Christmas Day 1941 sees Tom and his fellow comrades rescuing many members of both the Army and Navy from placements in and around the harbour until their ultimate capture by the Japanese, imprisonment under extremely harsh conditions, and eventual transportation on one of the infamous 'hell ships', the Lisbon Maru, which sails across the East China Sea bound for Japan with almost two thousand prisoners of war on board.

My account of the way Tom and his fellow prisoners of war were held and treated is set down with no malice towards the Japanese people, even though I find it difficult to understand their actions.

Events and stories of that time during the war in the Far East are presented as told to me and passed on by former Far East Prisoners of War, and researched from wartime records. Any errors in the book are mine. I have tried to include as much historical information as I was able to research.

Foreword

I never met Uncle Tom, my mother's brother, but I feel I know him through my mother Edna, who loved him, her stories of him and also through meeting Alf Hunt, a fellow prisoner of war with Tom held in captivity in Hong Kong by the Japanese in 1941 and 1942.

This is Tom's life – beginning in a loving happy Welsh home and living through days of hardship, loss and excitement, and finding strength and endurance against terrible odds.

Tom was the surviving baby of twin boys born in 1920. "Once a twin, always a twin" is a well-known phrase and studies have shown that a twin whose other twin dies in infancy possesses a built-in feeling that there is something missing in their lives and must strive to live for two. They find it difficult to talk about, but find comfort in talking to their mother about their feelings of loss and guilt about being the 'survivor'.

One

A list of 'draftees' is posted at the side of the parade ground for all to see. Officers and men of both the Royal Navy and Regular Army are included in this list, but they are subject to a strict medical in order to travel.

It is 7am on the twenty fifth of September 1942. Tom stands in one of the straight lines of men on the Jubilee parade ground at Sham Shui Po Camp, Hong Kong, and waits; beads of sweat on his forehead drip down into his eyes but he must keep still. The parade was assembled at 5.00am that morning and now the hot tropical sun is burning and intense. Flies, busy as always, buzz close to Tom's face but he must stand still and let them creep along his cheek towards his eye where they may find a little salty moisture to feed upon.

Then, at long last, a small Japanese officer comes out to address the parade in broken English. It is 7.30am. He tells the assembled group of British Prisoners of War, who number one thousand, eight hundred and sixty five, that they are about to "go to beautiful country, a better climate, do lots work, be good happy, keep busy!"

Tom, aged twenty-one, is just one of the assembled men who had been taken prisoner when the British colony of Hong Kong fell into Japanese hands on Christmas Day 1941, despite soldiers and sailors fighting to keep the colony in British control. Since then the prisoners have been held in appalling conditions with very little food and no news from the outside world as to their plight, or the outcome of the war raging in Europe. The Royal Navy is Tom's group and they number three hundred and sixty two men. Other groups around them include men from the Royal Artillery, Royal Scots Regiment and many smaller regiments all of whom were the surviving troops who had put up a brave fight to keep Hong Kong safe for Britain in whose domain it had been.

Now they all march forward and away from this hell that is Sham Shui Po Camp, their dreadful prison, down to the jetty at Bamboo Harbour and board a small boat which ferries them a group at a time over to a ship for the journey to Japan. The boat has to make several trips to get all one thousand, eight hundred and sixty five men on board. The ship has a painted name on its side both in English and Japanese "Lisbon Maru".

As they walk onto the jetty the men are sprayed with disinfectant and each man has already been vaccinated, numbered and photographed in the previous days. Now they are also issued with a kit bag containing fresh clothes, shoes, mess tin, blanket and overcoat. Many of the men are so weak from hunger, disease and maltreatment they struggle to carry the heavy kit bag. Again, as usual, the Japanese guards have little sympathy for those who fall behind, unable to march or carry any loads, and they are beaten with a wooden stick and told to keep up.

Tom and the Royal Navy prisoners are ordered into the ship's Number 1 Hold. He negotiates the long narrow metal ladder down into the hold where wooden shelves have been constructed down each side, and on the floor of the ship. At the bottom, on the keel, are sacks of sand. Tom sees his mate Alf ('Nobby') Hunt behind him and, as there is no more room in this hold, Nobby and the remaining sixteen of the Navy personnel are told to start filling Number 2 hold. Tom finds a small space with just room enough to sit down crammed between other men and leans against the kit bag. There is noisy chatter, amidst complaining about the cramped conditions, but also with a sense of slight excitement of actually being shipped out of the camp at last.

Tom is exhausted and closes his eyes. His mind is in a muddle and he worries about going to Japan. Will he ever get home again? Would his family know where he was? Despite the noise and heat and the three hundred or more men around him, his eyes are heavy and he drifts into sleep. His familiar dream comes to him and he is back in that small terraced house in South Wales when he was three years old in 1923 …

Two

Terraced houses in the street were mainly two bedroomed with a living room and a best front room or parlour downstairs. The parlour was rarely used whereas the living room was where the family cooked, ate, washed and where the small children played.

Tom drifted back to recall his earliest memories of that time, that house, and what was happening to him and his family in the depression of the 1920's in Wales.

He was playing with a piece of string when the sound of his mother's frantic coughing and struggling for breath suddenly stopped. It was the fourteenth of December 1923, just before Christmas, when the doctor came back down the stairs of the small terraced cottage in the town of Loughor to tell all eight children that their Mam had died. To Tom, only three years old, it seemed as though the world he was just beginning to get to know was sometimes quite scary. This was the second blow to befall him in his young life. He knew what the doctor was telling them, he knew the word 'death' – he had lost his twin brother Albert who had died from whooping cough when they were just fifteen months old. Tom had been very close to Albert and they had begun to chatter to each other with a few baby words followed by a game of crawling chase. The only fortunate consequence of being part of a large family was that he would be 'mothered' by, and find solace in, his sisters and brother.

His Mam had been ill for some considerable time, the birth

of Tom and Albert, the twins, in 1920 had been a difficult one requiring not just the local midwife but also the doctor in attendance as the second twin, Albert, was a breach birth (feet first, rather than head first) and took a long time to be born. Albert had also been much smaller than Tom and weighed only half that of his sibling. Before the age of scans, predicting that twins were expected was quite chancy. A midwife may be able to hear two heartbeats, but quite often the second baby arrived as a surprise. One more baby, a girl, was born a year and a half later in 1922 – it was the way things were in those days – a baby nearly every year, and brought the number of children she had borne to ten, not all of whom survived.

The children in order of birth were Minnie, Bertha, Ivy, Hilda, Nora, William, Gladys, Albert, Thomas and Edna.

The Gorseinon area of South Wales on an estuary close to the Bristol Channel has a rich historical past. Stone Age man and the Beaker People left their mark and when the Romans conquered South Wales in AD74 they stayed for 400 years leaving forts and roads. The old Swansea to Loughor road follows the straight line of the Roman road. The countryside is natural and beautiful and the seasons made themselves very keenly felt to the family. When the Normans took over the land in the twelfth century they built castles and churches which still stand today.

In 1904 Gorseinon became part of the great Welsh tin and steel manufacturing industry and this was enhanced when the first electrically-driven tinplate mill in the world was installed there that same year. The railway was in full service transporting the coal from the Welsh coalpits to the factories and smelting works both locally and nationally.

Wales had been kind to Tom's father, William, a gardener who had travelled from County Durham to Exeter in Devon to find work and there he met his wife, Fanny. They were married in Exeter in 1906 and lived in the St Thomas district of the city.

There was very little unskilled work to be found either gardening or labouring and so after their third baby girl was born they all moved to South Wales to the small town of Loughor, near Swansea, where it was possible for William to find some driving and labouring work and a house to rent.

The town had a lively mix of elementary and secondary schools, grassy slopes near the old castle which dated from Norman and Saxon times, and a boating club which held regattas in the summer on the wide Loughor River which flowed out into the Bristol Channel. This river has its source in the Black Mountains and marks the border between Carmarthenshire and Swansea. As it flows between Hendy and Pontarddulais it becomes tidal and meets the sea along the Gower Peninsula.

In the eighteenth century it was noted for its salmon and sea trout – the fish then being transported by pony to be sold at the Swansea market. The increasing pollution however, due to the rise in industrialisation in the nineteenth century, meant a decline in the fishing from the river. At low tide a wide sandy area is revealed where cockles are plentiful.

Theirs was a happy house, near the Chapel – full of singing at the weekends. Children were free to play in the streets and the older ones looked out for the youngest. The street was always lively and in the 1920's it was a hive of gossip as the housewives washed windows, scrubbed doorsteps and put the family prams outside to give the latest arrival some fresh air. Children's games were simple and involved whatever they could find in the way of rope for skipping, chalk for hopscotch markings, or small pebbles with which they would play 'five-stones', a game later known as 'jacks' – one stone was thrown up using one hand and with the same hand you had to pick up another stone and catch the first one as it fell.

The men of the family would gather in groups on the corner to talk, smoke, and wait for the wagon to pass picking up five or six men required for a day's labouring work on roads or buildings. The pubs, and there were quite a few, did well in the evenings when the men, tired from their labouring work all day, quenched their thirst with beer and cider, spending some of their hard earned money before they even got home. William was lucky in that he was taken on to drive a steam powered lorry in his local area for several months at a time.

What he had not realised though, when he moved his family to this area, was that this part of Wales had one of the highest mortality rates from tuberculosis (TB) thought to be caused by drinking unpasteurised milk (often having had unsuitable additives to prolong its shelf life) and also by droplet infection in the air. It is assumed that the Industrial North during the industrial revolution perhaps had a high death rate, but both Wales and South East England also had TB blackspots. Indeed the family was to lose two more children to the disease, one of whom was Tom's elder brother William, aged ten, in 1924 and his sister Gladys would die from TB in an open air sanatorium high in the Black Hills area of the Brecon Beacons at just seven years old.

Times were difficult, especially during the winter months when the house was so cold that frost would form on the insides of the windows upstairs. Men would collect coal from the railway sidings to feed their kitchen ranges which provided the only heat in their houses and a means of cooking. This fuel was free, within reason, to those who worked at the sidings and had to be collected in a wheelbarrow themselves. A brick, heated in the stove, would be wrapped in a piece of cloth and used to warm the bed before the children retired for the night.

There was no national health service and the services of a doctor had to be paid for. If a family was unable to afford the medical fees they could go to the local Magistrate's Court and apply for funds under the Poor Law, demeaning as it was, the only alternative was being taken into the care of the workhouse.

Tom pictured their small living room, which comprised kitchen, dining room and sitting room all in one. The range, or coal fired stove, was their source of heating and cooking and this iron stove, which was kept free from rust by applying black lead grate polish with a wet cloth, stayed alight all day throughout the year, and at night kept low – by covering the flames with a mixture of 'slack' which was coal-dust and water. Each morning the fire would be stirred into life again with sticks and coal. Tom loved the ritual of the fire, using the bellows when his mother asked him to get more air into the fire, or stirring it up with the poker under the watchful eye of elder siblings. If the fire went out, it had to be cleaned out and lit again with paper sticks made by folding newspaper into long strips and twisting them, then a few pieces of wood and then coal. Tom remembered his father leaning down holding a large piece of newspaper across the front of the fire to draw the air in from below the grate. This practice was quite risky as the paper would be drawn into the flames much to Tom's delight.

The coal bucket was constantly being filled from the coalhouse at the back of the house, supplied by father using his wheelbarrow to get coal from the local railway sidings – a perk he was allowed while he worked there. Next to the coalhouse was a small 'privvy' or toilet and the adjoining cold room was where the family would store the carcass of a pig they had raised, hanging on an iron spike after the local butcher had slaughtered it. None of the pig was wasted, the head was boiled to make brawn, the trotters were cooked and the meat carefully picked out.

The kitchen table was always in use. Here was the area for food preparation, writing letters, sewing or just sitting down to meals and to talk. There was always plenty to talk about – gossip from callers at the front door and street, news from the local shop or school, stories from the newspapers both national and local. There was always laughter. Each street would have a local 'character' who would get into trouble or do daft things. Callers to the house would always be welcomed with a cup of tea from the constantly simmering kettle on the hearth while they told their versions of the latest gossip and news. Oil lamps lit the room and a candle would light the way up to bed at night.

Mostly every day except Sunday, the day of rest, was very busy. With nine children and father working on the road gangs it meant filthy clothes and boots at the end of his shift, no modern appliances to help with washing, cleaning and cooking and so it was a full time job to do all the housework. The older girls were put to work either helping with the washtub or looking after the younger siblings. There would be a housebound neighbour needing their shopping done too.

Sleeping arrangements were quite difficult for a large family and children had to sleep 'top to toe' several to a bed. With a pillow at both the head and the foot of the bed, one child slept one way and the next slept with their feet by the first one's head. It could take quite a while for the children to settle down to sleep, either due to fighting for bed space or due to talking and laughing.

Friendship mattered and help was given where necessary. Even as Tom dozed, he felt warm and comfortable with the memories.

At school there was always music and singing, and in particular the song "Land of my Fathers". The words had been written in 1856 by Evan James with the tune having been composed a little earlier by his son James James while he walked beside the River Rhondda. Both had lived in Pontypridd, Glamorganshire.

This song was adopted by the Welsh Rugby Union in 1905 in response to the New Zealand's team traditional 'Hacka' at their match at Cardiff Arms Park. The memorial statue captures Evan and James at the Ynysangharad Park, Pontypridd and is known as "Poetry and Music".

The first verse in English is:

"This land of my fathers is dear to me
Land of poets and singers and people of stature
Her brave warriors, fine patriots
Shed their blood for freedom"

Nothing can be more moving than to hear the whole crowd in a stadium singing the anthem in Welsh.

As soon as the weather allowed, playing outside was permitted in the street, the park or the favourite small beach nearby. The beach was beside the Loughor Bridge – a railway viaduct joining Swansea and Llanelli, making a short cut for train travellers rather than having to make the long journey inland and out again. Originally designed by Isambard Kingdom Brunel in 1852, the viaduct was a timber construction with a small swing section to let shipping through.

The 'sea' as Tom remembered it was an ever widening estuary which emptied the river into the Bristol Channel and then the Atlantic and it was tidal. Tom recalled they had no watches or idea of the time they spent playing but when the tide rose and covered most of the beach it was a warning to get home.

Tom was watching his father in the kitchen mending shoes on the 'last' – a metal stand which was shaped like a foot over which the shoe could be put and a new sole nailed on – tap, tap, tap ...

Three

Morse Code is usually transmitted by lights or signals, but it can also be done skilfully by tapping on metal – the taps being heard at quite a distance. The code uses dots and dashes and tapping out one tap for the dot and three taps in quick succession for the dash it is possible to make up the coded words.

The tapping becomes hammering on metal. Tom wakes to realise he is in the bowels of a ship crowded with his fellow captives, men who are signalling with Morse code that they need water, need a toilet, need food.

The ship is the Lisbon Maru, a Japanese freighter built for the Yokohama Dock Company and launched in 1920. Her Captain is Kyoda Shigeru.

The British Commanding Officer in charge of both Hold 1 and Hold 2 is Lieutenant Colonel Stewart of the Middlesex Regiment (fondly nicknamed 'Monkey Stewart'). He is trying to keep order and calm. He negotiates with the Japanese captain to let the men (five at a time) go up on deck to use the latrines which are planks of wood on ropes slung over the side of the ship. Needless to say, men who are sick from the ravages of the poor diet and conditions they had endured in the camps cannot wait their turn for the latrine and are weak with various ailments, soon the floor of the hold becomes a stinking morass of vomit and bodily waste. There is only a small dim light in the hold when the hatches are closed, the rats scurry about and flies and biting insects do their worst. Will this ever end? Everyone is calling out or tapping a Morse code message, asking for information, wondering when the ship will raise anchor and move on to the next phase of their lives.

A very thin fellow prisoner next to Tom is moaning and sweating profusely. Tom watches him for a few minutes and realises he is watching him die. There is no time to lose, the man has no doubt died of an infectious disease and will need to be removed from the hold. His thoughts are correct and this man and seven more who show signs of diphtheria are taken off the ship. It seems the longer they wait to set off the fewer prisoners will survive to work in Japan.

There is suddenly an order for a roll-call. All scramble up the narrow metal ladder and onto the deck where it is much cooler. Every man is handed out soup and rice in their mess tins and half a loaf of bread. Perhaps in Japan there will be medicines for them if they are to be workers – as they have promised – and a decent diet and clean water. Workers need good health to provide the work the country would require ...

Four

Tuberculosis is caused by infection with an organism called the 'tubercle bacillus' and can affect most organs and tissues of the body producing lesions, both acute and chronic; the bacillus having been ingested, inhaled or absorbed through the skin by handling infected material.

Tom was taking gulps of the fresher air on the deck of the ship and was able to rest against an open hatch cover. He was again going back to that familiar dream as his eyes closed, and to his childhood …

The dream always seemed to start with that memorable day when he was three years old.

The doctor made his way slowly and carefully down the narrow staircase, rehearsing in his mind what to say to them, and he paused on the bottom step behind the door that led to the kitchen. He had been their family doctor since they had moved to the area and he had built up a good rapport with them. The kitchen was warm and cosy in the crisp December morning sunshine and the black-leaded range was well stoked up with coal and had the large black kettle 'singing' on top ready for making cups of tea. A large cooked ham and fresh loaf of bread were on the immaculate white tablecloth which covered the big old table used for all meals.

A light fall of snow had made everything in the room brighter and the usual friendly robin was bouncing about on the windowsill eagerly eating the few crumbs of bread put out for him. Opening the window just slightly allowed enough room to put the crumbs on the windowsill. The robin was so tame he would sometimes hop through the window opening and onto the inside sill – much to father's anger. Superstition was strongly felt, and a robin coming indoors might signal a death in that house. The bread was put out quickly before the robin had his chance to come in. Tom, ever the clown, pretended to be the robin, pecking at pretend crumbs and made them all laugh. There seemed to be so many superstitions which were drummed into the children – never put shoes on the table; don't cut your nails on a Friday; never cross knives on the table, and if you spilled salt you had to pick up a pinch with your right hand and throw it over your left shoulder. Salt has, since ancient Roman times, been a symbol of friendship and a very valuable commodity – the soldiers were paid in salt (from the Latin 'salary'). The belief that spilling it brings bad luck is perpetuated in the bible story that Judas Iscariot spilled it at the Last Supper. Some of these beliefs were sensible though and could possibly save accidents. Not passing someone on the stairs, and never walking under a ladder were examples of these.

All these stories and worry about bad luck seemed to have been either ancient folklore or tales put about by the travelling gypsies who would call at the door to sell 'lucky' heather – and if you failed to buy a bunch you felt you may have incurred a curse on the house! It seemed the more stories that were heard the more things were unlucky. Seeing a white horse in a field was bad luck, unless you wet your finger and touched your shoe with it. Peacock feathers were never to be brought into the house and woe betide anyone who opened an umbrella indoors.

The fairground was in full swing in May and September in the town and the travelling people made their money on the stalls and rides. There was also a small tent where 'Gypsy Rose

Lee' would tell fortunes using a crystal ball or by reading your palm.

But now the subdued feeling returned and everyone was quiet this morning, they knew the doctor was upstairs and all of them hoped he could make their mother better again. Their father had come down from the bedroom already and was preparing the teacups on the table. It was certainly quiet upstairs and now the door to the staircase slowly opened. The doctor cleared his throat and said "Well, I did all I could, but your mammy was too ill to go on in this life. You will all have to help your daddy now. I am sorry …"

Tom held his father's hand as the doctor spoke softly to them all. Their father who had his other arm around Nora's shoulders, as she was just five years old, listened quietly. Edna, the youngest, who was just eighteen months old thought the 'story' the doctor was telling them all was a moment to enjoy and giggled. Her father gave her a sharp tap on the hand and told her to be silent which then of course made her cry.

The quiet moment had gone and the doctor's soothing voice changed into a more commanding one telling them all to be strong and to help their Daddy with everything – "Lend a hand with all the chores, be good at school and do as you are told". How often had this young doctor been in similar households saying the same words to a bereaved family is unclear, but these were the days before counselling was widely thought of as a healing process, before vaccination programmes dealt with the misery of TB (tuberculosis), and other childhood illnesses, and the family doctor took on the role without question.

Tom's father already knew the heartbreaking news of course. He had been upstairs by his wife's side as her face turned blue through lack of the oxygen she so badly needed and could no longer breathe into her lungs. As she slipped into unconsciousness her brave battle with 'the consumption', as TB was also known, was over and he had kissed her forehead. Slowly now there began stifled sobbing and questions being asked by the younger ones who tugged at the sleeves of the older ones for answers.

Tom stood still by the table, surveying the room with his steely grey-blue eyes, wishing he was taller, bigger than his three years allowed. He knew he wanted to be good and help his daddy and all of them because they had helped him by talking about his own twin brother Albert. There was even a photograph of him with Albert on their mother's lap – he looked at the picture now up there on the high mantelpiece and knew he would always be reminded of Albert and now his mammy too.

The doctor gratefully took a cup of tea and was talking to father now about the arrangements which would be made for his wife. The district nurse would be coming in to lay her out. He would have to contact the undertaker himself, and it would be likely the burial would have to wait until after Christmas. The doctor left the small terraced house by the front door which led directly onto the pavement, icy now after the frosty night. He stood in silence for a few moments and took a deep breath of the cold air. He wondered how this cruel epidemic that was TB would ever be beaten. It was well known that fresh air and good food helped patients to recover, but more than anything there needed to be a cure.

As he moved away from the house the older girls were already closing the curtains to the front windows. This was a tradition everywhere at that time and it let the neighbours know there had been a death in that house, as well as 'closing out the world' during the family's grieving process. When the nurse came that evening to wash their mother and put on a white shroud, the undertaker had already brought a coffin and placed it on trestle stands in the front parlour and now, with his assistant, he carried her down and placed her in the coffin which was draped in a sheet. It was considered quite normal for a family member who had died to be laid out in the parlour – the best and rarely used cold room at the front of the house. The family would live in the back room where they cooked, ate, bathed and dried their clothes by the heat of the fire.

After a week of silence and tears in that small house, and a rather sombre Christmas which their father tried to make as good as possible for the small children, the undertaker came to screw down the coffin lid but, before he did, William gathered all the children in the front parlour to say goodbye to their mother and give her a kiss. The little ones had to be lifted up to reach their mummy's cold face. "Bye Mam" they each said to her. Toddlers and teenagers alike, they all managed to pay their last respects to their poor mother. This ritual was always adhered to and was thought to be a valuable part of the mourning process. All of them had their Sunday best clothes on, the girls wore their white starched and frilled pinafore aprons over their best dresses and the boys had good shirts which had been made for them by a neighbour who earned a little money for her sewing skills.

Five

Mourners walked behind the funeral cortege, wearing black to show their respect for the family and their loss.

The day of the funeral came and the slow walk behind the horse drawn hearse was a quiet and sombre one, apart from the odd word of comfort from neighbours watching from the roadside as they passed by. It was January and their special day for their mother was a bitterly cold, grey one, with some snow on the roadsides and grave tops. There was no sun or blue sky and the sea mist had crept up from the estuary and across the long bridge which divided their village from the main town. Their breath steamed in the cold air and added to the mist.

Tom held his father's hand and felt proud that he was by his father's side. William thanked those who had made the small Chapel so beautiful for the day. There were strips of ivy and laurel decorating the front pews and a few late winter roses which had been given from their neighbour's garden and were placed on the coffin. Prayers were said and hymns sung and the coffin was lowered into the waiting grave amid many tears.

After the service back in the kitchen at home over cups of tea their father allowed himself a few silent tears. He was strong, but he missed his wife terribly, and was at a loss to know what to do now that he was left alone to raise his children, he knew it would be difficult to find even driving work in what was becoming known as the 'recession' and earn the much needed money to buy food for all nine of them, and buy coal for the hungry black range to cook on and keep them warm.

It was January 1924 and men still stood on street corners hoping to be taken on for a few hours labouring work or queued at the offices of the local coal pit for work. It was this that occupied his thoughts even on the funeral day. The answer came in the form of a young woman who answered the family's request for help through the vicar of the chapel. The girl was eighteen years old and loved caring for children, and she was taken on to help William to look after the little ones. The eldest two daughters were growing up into capable young ladies and would soon be starting jobs of their own and would not be there to chivvy along the little ones, dress them, feed them and get them to school.

Just a year later in 1924, Tom's older brother Willie died aged just ten years old, from pulmonary TB. Once more the family coped with the funeral arrangements and sadness. Life had to go on even in those dark days and, although devastated at his son's death, William made the most of family gatherings around that kitchen table and talked with them all whenever he could, making sure they all knew they were loved and cared for.

In 1925 William met and fell in love with a young lady called Mary, and very soon the family had a new stepmother, a big change for the children missing their mother's care and missing their father too, as he was now back out at full time work again.

Again the bad luck was not to go away and William's daughter Gladys, aged seven, died from TB later that same year of 1925 whilst being nursed at the Adelina Patti Hospital in the Black Hills of Brecon.

So it was among these tragic times that Tom began his fifth year of childhood and, in a family of mainly girls; six sisters and himself, he was cherished and grew up quickly in such a busy, but happy, home.

Six

School days began when the hand bell was rung in
the playground and all children were to line up ready
to walk quietly into the school hall for assembly

The eldest girls loved dressing and feeding the 'babbies' as the younger ones were known and would sometimes walk the youngsters to school. Tom loved his small elementary school – not so much for the provision of education, but more for the companionship and fun of being in a large group of boys and girls all his age. Long wooden forms were used to sit on in class and slates and pencils used to write with. The teacher would write on a blackboard with chalk.

Prayers were said before classes began and a hymn was sung. It was forbidden to speak Welsh at school, despite many of the children using that language at home. This had been a political decision governing education from the early nineteenth century as it was thought to hinder a child's learning. Those who lapsed into speaking in Welsh were punished and made an example of, with time spent standing on a stool at the front of class with a wooden sign with 'WN' painted on it. This stood for 'Welsh Not' and the sign would be passed on to any other pupil who forgot what they were saying and spoke in Welsh. Traditionally, the pupil who was wearing the sign at the end of the day would have a beating.

The Welsh language evolved from Brittonic, or indigenous

Breton, as opposed to Anglo Saxon, and it was spoken in both Wales and England until the Romans came along.

In the 1940's there was a profound change in thinking about the Welsh language and to preserve the national tongue Welsh Medium Schools were introduced where it was acceptable to have lessons mainly in Welsh, with pupils becoming bi-lingual. Demand for these schools increased over the following decades.

In Tom's school books at were all in English and all lessons given using English. In the 1920's school was a harsh and disciplined place, but perhaps it built hardy characters, able to withstand the knocks that adult life would bring. Children would walk home for dinner at midday and back again by 1.30pm for lessons in the afternoon. Teachers would be addressed as 'Sir' or 'Miss'.

Tom was outgoing and had a big personality (his way of compensating for his missing twin perhaps), always excelling at sport and games. He was not a born scholar though and left school with few qualifications academically.

His one great passion throughout his childhood and teenage years was the small seashore near his home where he and one or two of his sisters would love to spend hours playing. Tom dreamt now of his beach which was a sandy, stony strip edging the wide estuary of the river which made its way out to the Atlantic. It was tidal and at high tide the beach was well under water. The children were given strict warnings to get home before the tide came up the beach, and in October when the days grew shorter and the tides were faster and higher they could no longer go there to play until spring came again.

Plenty of warnings were issued to them all at home in September about the approaching 'October tides' and their play time in Autumn and Winter would be restricted to the streets and indoors.

All summer Tom would imagine he was one of the sailors or

pirates he read about and would make pretend telescopes from cardboard to look far out to sea and then tell his playmates to hide as the pirates were coming ashore! The girls collected shells and 'cooked' seaweed on pretend stoves on the beach, while Tom got a stick and drew out complicated diagrams of ships on the sand. If there was some mess left by a dog they would point and shout in Welsh "Ych y fi!" (pronounced 'ukka vee' meaning Ugh!), quickly learnt by the small children and always fun to shout. Tom kept his siblings amused – he was a born joker with a wicked smile and as he grew into a teenager had a wink which could bring a blush to a girl's cheeks.

Seven

*Wales became one of the world's most depressed
countries – unemployment reaching 42% by 1932.
Not just coal, but steel, tinplate, slate, transport and
agriculture were all affected by the slump. This resulted
in mass emigration, poor diet, housing and health.*

There followed the years of Tom's growing up in the
1930's, helping his father tend the pigs and geese kept in
the back yard. There was always a good supply of salted pork
and ham. Large eggs supplied by the geese, and of course the
geese themselves were used as meat. The small scullery behind
the kitchen was cool enough to keep a couple of butchered pigs
hanging ready for use. Vegetables were grown where the soil
was good enough. The four eldest girls Minnie, Bertha, Ivy and
Hilda went into needlework, waitressing work or into 'service'
for a grand house as soon as they were sixteen and were at home
most weekends with lots of stories to tell.

Edna, the youngest daughter, was admitted to the Adalina
Patti open air sanatorium in the hills of Brecon in 1928 at
the age of six where she was nursed for three years as she had
developed TB in her intestines. She was nursed on a plaster cast
fixed to her bed which was then pushed out onto the balcony for
the day in all weathers – in winter and summer, rain and sun.
As she recovered she had to learn to walk again by holding onto
her beside locker and pushing it along the ward. Her beloved

toy doll bought on the journey there by bus and train for a few pennies became a substitute for her family who were rarely able to visit her. She loved the kind nurses who cared for her and longed to be a nurse herself when she grew up. Edna recovered and, on returning home from hospital aged nine, her first chore was to beat the mats on the line – clouds of dust settling on her clothes. The year was 1931.

William worked hard and found jobs where he could to earn enough money. He was taken on for a few months at a time driving the steam lorry which delivered tarmac to make good the roads. Coal was plentiful and steam lorries were reasonably cheap to run. When he had surplus meat or eggs to sell he made a bit of spare cash too.

The harsh winter of 1934 descended over the country like a wet veil and brought colds, flu and disease with it. William caught pneumonia and died in 1935 thin and pale – so the head of the family was sadly taken from them all. The Chapel was once more decorated with flowers and greenery for the funeral service – full of hymns sung by the family and friends. Life in Wales was now untenable for such a large family, now almost grown up, and the family was now an extended one as there were stepsisters and stepbrothers to look out for.

Minnie and Ivy stayed in South Wales where they lived and worked and where they both found caring husbands to love and marry. Hilda moved first – to Devon where she had found a job, and Bertha too went to Exeter in Devon where she stayed with her aunt, (their mother's sister) and found work locally. Tom, Edna and Norah soon followed and settled in Devon.

Eight

The rich arable land in Devon attracted workers from the north of England and Wales and Ireland where conditions were difficult. New roads and waterway links added to the more productive lifestyle and healthier conditions.

At the start of 1937 Tom was almost eighteen and had grown into a fine young man. He was working as a hall porter in a hotel in Exeter, a job he was lucky to get, and over the last two years had built up a good set of muscles from carrying all the heavy suitcases and bags to and from the guest's rooms. This was a job with little prospect of becoming either permanent or well paid. He would start very early in the morning setting out the newspapers in the reception and lounge areas, or delivery some to the guest's rooms. The tips he received often exceeded his pay packet and he was able to save a bit and contribute to living expenses at home.

Hailing taxis when a guest was leaving and taking the luggage out to the taxi or using a hand truck to wheel it all across to the main railway station kept him busy and he got on well with the Head Porter in whose command he was. He enjoyed the work however and worked long shifts becoming an expert on customer service. His local knowledge of the city and the area around the hotel was invaluable and he loved talking to the guests when he could, advising them about local sights to see, and he delighted in hearing their tales of travels to foreign countries. "Where are you off to next?" Tom would ask the owner of a large suitcase. The reply he got was usually "Canada – I'm going to be a settler!" or "America to stay with relatives." He dreamt about seeing some of those places one day.

Maybe it was handling all the luggage destined for foreign shores, his love of the sea as a child, the uniform, or maybe the need for a more exciting life, Tom decided to join the Navy. "Tour The World – Join The Royal Navy" and "This is the Life" posters in the town announced. It was easier than he had expected as there was a new recruitment drive and registration system in progress, and he went to the recruiting office to get started. There was a long form to be filled in by the recruitment officer asking all sorts of questions which Tom answered as well as he could. How would he fare in hot tropical weather conditions? Could he swim? Would he stay the course and finish his training?

After his very thorough medical examination, teeth check and eye test he waited for his call up papers. He signed on for twelve years and after two months of agonised waiting a letter arrived in an official brown envelope marked 'On His Majesty's Service' which told Tom he had been accepted and to report to HMS Drake at Devonport, Plymouth on 9 May to start his formal training to become a Stoker in the Royal Navy.

There were a few days to wait and Tom, Norah and Edna decided to catch the bus to Ilfracombe, North Devon, and then the paddle steamer Glyn Gower over to Swansea to visit Ivy, their eldest sister and her husband Alfred. This had to be a 'flying visit' as Tom was now quite close to leaving for his new career and had to sort out a lot of paperwork, packing and making arrangements at home. But the day was very enjoyable and Ivy was the perfect hostess with plenty of food and drink flowing.

After a huge lunch it was time to go back down to the quay to catch the ferry and the return trip to Devon. Tom loved the ferry boat and it increased his excitement at the thought that he would soon be working on board a large ship somewhere. The movement of the boat bobbing at the quayside brought Tom back to the present and he wakes up lying on the cool upper deck …

Nine

Captive prisoners of war made the best of the situation they found themselves in, telling jokes, writing diaries, singing and reminiscing.

It is evening on the twenty seventh of September 1942 on board the Lisbon Maru – and after queuing to use the latrine Tom is making the most of the wonderful cool air and sea breeze on deck. The temperature down in the hold is unbearable and with the hatches closed there is no respite from the heat. The body itself is continuously producing its own heat as a by-product of metabolism which is the process when food is converted into energy or growth.

The body has three ways of self-cooling and the first is to slow down metabolism which in turn produces less heat. The second method happens as more blood is circulated to the periphery of the body where it should be cooled naturally. Sweating is the third method of cooling, and in those conditions the sweat would pour from the prisoners in their hot confinement, but the humid air around them would prevent the sweat from evaporating and cooling the skin. Heat exhaustion is therefore commonplace amongst the men and in severe cases heatstroke which is much more serious. The body temperature can reach 40 degrees centigrade or higher, and this causes confusion, fits and loss of consciousness and eventual death. Several men died from heatstroke despite being lifted by several of the men onto the deck to cool them down. The guards dealt with the dead bodies by slipping them over the side of the ship on planks acting as a slide; the sharks in the sea only too ready to receive them.

Tom is ordered back down into the hold. The metal ladder fixed to the side wall is difficult and very slippery with sweat and other bodily fluids. More sick prisoners have been sent back ashore and there is renewed hope that today the ship will set sail.

To pass the time there is quite a lot of singing – someone even has a small accordion, or squeeze-box, to play. Many smutty jokes are told and passed around. Some who have paper and pencil are writing diaries or playing quiz games. Tom is comforted by the humour and stoicism of his mates and a few hours later he is again asleep and dreaming of his life so far …

Ten

On 17th May 1587 Francis Drake wrote "There must be a begynnyng of any great matter, but the contenewing unto the end untyll it be thoroughly ffynyshed yeldes the trew glory." This extract from his letter was made into a prayer in 1941 by the Dean of York, the prayer has since been called 'Drake's Prayer'.

Tom recalled the day in May 1938 which arrived at last when he was to join his barracks and Tom took his travel pass to the railway ticket office where he was given a train ticket from Exeter St Davids Station to his training establishment in Plymouth. After emotional scenes at the railway station saying goodbye to his family, and a strict warning from his elder sister about not getting any girls into trouble, he was off.

Tom made friends easily and he was able to hand out a few cigarettes to lads on the train journey to Plymouth, some of whom were also joining up. The start of a new life was forming for Tom and he laughed and joked with his mates as they walked from the station to the naval barracks. There is a moment that stays in the mind always. Such a moment happened for Tom as they arrived at the gatehouse – the gateway to his new life. Tom and his group of new recruits stood open-mouthed at the sight of the buildings as they walked through the entrance gatehouse. Large Victorian stone walls, high windows and wonderful stone carvings were taken in as they walked through to the large forecourt. So this was HMS Drake. Tom had learnt about Sir

Francis Drake at school and was thrilled by the stories of his adventures. The Barracks in Devonport, close to Plymouth, were named HMS Drake in 1934 in honour of the famous Plymouth man. Before that however, twenty three sea-going ships had borne the name 'Drake', the first in 1588 was privately owned by Francis Drake who came from a wealthy family. Commanded by Captain Henry Spindelow she played a vital role in the campaign of the Spanish Armada taking part in battles off Plymouth, Portland and the Isle of Wight. When the Spanish were anchored off Calais, the Drake was sent in as a 'fireship', fully ablaze, all sails set, drifting slowly on the incoming tide towards Calais harbour. Many Spaniards cut their anchor cables and fled. Thus they were defeated.

The new conscripts were given talks on the history of HMS Drake, and would have had access to the library which held not only books on the subject, but memorabilia such as Drake's ceremonial drum. The following twenty two ships which were named Drake were mainly gun ships taking part in various campaigns worldwide. The eighth Drake, a fourteen gun vessel was built at Bombay in 1736 – a two hundred ton ship with a crew of ninety four. She took part in a major operation resulting in the overthrow of the notorious pirate – Tulagee Angria. The twenty third Drake was launched at Pembroke, Wales in 1901. She was an eighteen gun cruiser and in 1905, whilst in Portsmouth Dockyard, His Majesty King Edward VII visited the ship and spent the night on board. Drake was then involved in naval action during World War One and in October 1917 was torpedoed off the coast of Ireland, managing to reach harbour before sinking in shallow water. She was the last ship to bear the name of Drake and the name was not used again until it was given to the Barracks.

Plymouth had attracted naval activity as early as 1442 when eight ships patrolled the area during the time attacks were anticipated from the French. Merchant adventurers assembled crews for their ships in Plymouth prior to discovering new lands. As a child, Francis Drake was brought by his parents to Plymouth during a period of civil unrest and they sheltered on St Nicholas Island – later renamed 'Drake's Island'. Francis remained in the South West and began working on merchant ships, his first voyage to the Americas was in 1563 with his cousin, John Hawkins, whose family in Plymouth owned a fleet of ships. By 1588 Drake had risen to Vice Admiral of the English Fleet and this was when he defeated the Spanish Armada. Whether he had been playing bowls on Plymouth Hoe as the Spanish approached is not confirmed, but the popular myth is that Drake said he had time to finish the game and still beat the Spanish!

Tom and his comrades joined a queue, the first of many, to be signed in, issued with kit and uniform and given a stern talk about the rules to be strictly followed. Each man was expected to keep fit, exercise and eat and sleep well. A high-energy diet was provided with three good meals a day.

They would be woken at 6.00am, their 6.15am breakfast would be followed by a talk from the Commander outlining the training routine and orders they had to follow. Their kit included a cylindrical canvas bag which held a hammock. This, as was explained, you had to sling each night at your own assigned space with hooks attached to the hammock bar above them and then lashed. Tom was installed in a dormitory which had space for 50 recruits and found his number and space where there was a locker to store his kit.

Among much hilarity and with difficulty, each put on his new uniform ready for their first inspection. Their commanding officer walked up and down the line of new faces and put several mistakes right where the separate collars needed attention or trousers would need to be adjusted. He told them that all their kit including their billet would be clean and tidy, their hammock was to be folded and stored in their lockers each morning before roll call at 6.00am. They were told where the laundry room was and the washing was done in large stone sinks with soap and scrubbing brushes, and the wet clothes were hung over a line to dry.

Ironing had to be done correctly so that all uniforms looked exactly alike. The bell bottomed trousers were made of rough navy blue serge and they had a thinner pair for 'best'. The trousers had to be kept folded ready for use in the kit bag and were stored inside out to avoid shine when ironing. They were ironed by folding them horizontally at a hand's width and then taped into a rectangular block. When opened out therefore and turned the right side out, they would have inverted vertical creases down the side of each leg and seven horizontal creases down each leg (five creases if the man was shorter).

After being given the signal to fall out, they were then free to get to know the barracks and find the canteen for a cooked tea. In the Mess a supper of mutton stew and potatoes followed by rice pudding was hungrily eaten by all and back on the verandah of their hut they talked and smoked, swapped stories of their lives and home towns and girlfriends until the order came to put their hammocks up before lights out.

There was a tradition Tom soon learnt that almost everyone had a nickname – usually related in some way to their surname. Amongst much hilarity, the men heard the names "Spud" Murphy, "Dicky" Bird, "Bunny" Warren and "Shady" Lane. Plymouth itself was always referred to as "Guzz" and if there was anything a nickname could be tagged onto, it was.

The barracks were well appointed with a large dining hall, swimming pool, skittles alley and even a sick bay. The laundry was done by the ratings in the basement at sinks by hand. Water which overflowed the sinks ran into gullies down each side of the laundry room. So began Tom's initial training period of three weeks. This would be followed by five weeks of technical training designed for those who would become a Stoker. Leave was granted every other day and evening cinema leave was usually granted. A weekend once a month from noon on Saturday until Sunday night was the rule. The pay was fourteen shillings a week, with extra allowance paid if a first aid qualification was gained.

The small beach in South Wales next to the
Loughor Viaduct where Tom played as a child.

HMS Drake, Plymouth.

HMS Drake Laundry, Plymouth.

Tom in Royal Navy Uniform – this photograph was taken as Tom began his tour of duty in Hong Kong in 1939, aged nineteen. Each new rating on HMS Tamar waited in a queue at the Kwong Lom Studio to have their photograph taken, a copy being sent home to his family. A study of a keen young man, proudly wearing his uniform expertly ironed with a central crease in the shirt-front, full of eagerness and anticipation that his blossoming career promised. Hair perfectly 'Brylcreemed' in the fashionable style of the day. Clean shaven, fresh faced, lips only just hiding a smile and showing perfect teeth. His eyes seem to shine and are ready to wink with that slight turn of head he was known for.

HMS Tamar, Shore Base, Hong Kong.

Tom in his Number Six white uniform on board HMS Thracian.

*HMS Thracian in Hong Kong. The ship Tom worked
on during his time in Hong Kong.*

The Lisbon Maru.

The Sinking of The Lisbon Maru map.

The author with Alf Hunt, a fellow Royal Navy prisoner of war with Tom, the photograph was taken in Birmingham at a COFEPOW meeting on 16 August 2011.

Eleven

"Since sea air and training will keep your appetite keen, it might be as well here and now to take a look at a typical day's menu: Breakfast – porridge, bacon and tomatoes, marmalade. Dinner – Soup, roast meat, baked potatoes, peas, suet pudding and jam. Tea – Bread, margarine, jam, tea. Supper – Soused herring, bread, margarine, tea."

(Quotation taken from HM Government's "Joining Up" booklet issued in 1938).

Never had there been such long or tiring days as were now experienced by Tom and his mates. He had thought the porter's job had been hard work, but here you had to work hard mentally as well as physically. A timetable of rifle drill, PE, semaphore training, first aid training, parade ground marching drill, spud bashing and cleaning duties had to be strictly adhered to. Tutorials were given by the qualified sailors on naval protocol, flags, signalling etc, etc. Tom did well at the first aid classes and qualified as a first aider in just a few months.

There was a whole new vocabulary to learn too. Most of it was slang. Officers, they learned, also had nicknames. The Padre was usually referred to as the "Sky Pilot" while there were further surnames to learn which always attracted an extra description such as 'Dusty Miller', 'Nobby Clark', 'Smudger Smith' or 'Rocky Stone'. Swearing was the norm too, although frowned upon by the officers and sometimes punished with extra duties.

More Navy terminology was continually being passed around the ranks, such as 'Ab-Dab' – a Stoker's term for an Able Seaman (an AB whose job it was to DAB paint on things!); a 'Doofer' – a half-smoked cigarette (do-fer later!).

Tom enjoyed all the sporting activities during his time there. With other naval training schools in nearby Devonport and Portsmouth there were plenty of chances to play an opposing team at football or running, and best of all were the tug of war competitions which Tom's team usually, but not always, won.

Six weeks of intense training drew to a close with a light hearted rowing competition in the harbour at which Tom's crew won and were awarded the prize of a few beers each in the Mess that night. Each newly qualified Naval Rating was then given a few days leave before they were to join their designated ship where their real career was to start.

Tom got the mid-morning train from Plymouth to Exeter to spend his leave with his sisters and aunt. On the journey, which was slow, he had time to reflect on the last few weeks and how much he had learned and achieved. He compared his life now to the life he had lived as a child in Wales. The cramped living conditions with eleven of them living in what was only really a 'two up, two down' house had been both challenging and great fun.

Never had there been many quiet moments, or times of boredom and of course there had been his beloved days at the seashore and the long bridge where he could gaze out to sea and dream. There were only two bedrooms at the house and one of those was his mum and dad's. The other contained three beds where siblings slept top to toe and where he and his older brother Will had played tricks by putting a fir cone in their sister's bed or folding the sheets into an 'apple pie bed' to surprise the occupants. The top sheet would be folded so as not to allow your legs to go right down the bed length – the fold causing your feet to stop suddenly, and usually painfully!

Baths were taken in a large tin bath in the outhouse in the summer or beside the kitchen fire in winter. They had only the basic items required to live comfortably but it had been a happy household with singing and laughter – especially when his father came home with his pay-packet. Then they would plan what to spend and what to save in the pot on the mantelpiece. There were always pennies for the younger ones to spend on sweets at Gwyn's shop on the corner. Nearly every town trader had a special name which was usually the shop owner's surname followed by his trade. Therefore there would be 'Gwyn the Sweets', 'Jenkins the Garage', 'Davey the Bread' and so on. Tom smiled at his memories as he watched the endless Devon fields from the train window.

The kitchen in Wales had always been warm and welcoming and there had been plenty of food to eat. He thought back now with fondness on those days, and with sadness at his mother's parting. He could picture her still with a loaf of bread tucked in her arm against her apron cutting off slices towards her and wondering how there had not been more accidents with knives.

Tom often wondered what his twin brother Albert would have been like. Maybe he would have joined the Navy too. Twins share not only their emotions and pain (it is well documented that even when miles apart, one twin will feel pain in the same area of the body as the other twin is experiencing), but they share between them various traits such as offloading to their other twin, by unspoken agreement, their exuberance, anger, wickedness etc while keeping the traits they want – such as quietness, solitude, keen learning. This sharing out seems to occur during their very early years and usually levels out as they grow and have to learn to conform at school.

A case study was made of twin boys in Devon in the 1980s.

The twins were six years old. Timothy was placid, kind and keen to learn while Jeremy was impetuous, daredevil and always the practical joker, sometimes playing dangerous tricks on people. They played well together however, leaving the other to his path in life with something akin to relief that either the 'good' or 'naughty' element was being played out by the sibling twin.

Therefore each twin in his own right must ostensibly be a more intense character as he can concentrate more fully on his favourite feelings and ideas for himself. When Tom lost Albert just as they were developing this sharing out of characteristics it would have left Tom feeling extra bereft not only of their close tactile bond, but of Albert's growing awareness of what type of twin he would be. Tom knew he had to live for them both and took on the doubly difficult task of his twin's emotions and traits himself.

The visit home passed quickly and much was talked about, including the impending possibility of war with Germany. Tom reassured them all that with him in the Navy all would be well, much to their amusement. There was a table full of food to be eaten, tea to drink and jugs of beer when they wanted. Tom fell into bed tired but happy knowing that tomorrow his life would really be beginning.

Twelve

In Navy slang Stokers were known as the 'Black Gang' due to their work in the engine room liberally in contact with coal, oil and grease.

Tom was now qualified as a Leading Stoker, and he listened intently as the roll call was made. This one was not only to check all personnel had returned to the barracks on time, but after each group of ten names were called the destination for those names was also read out.

Tom and his allotted group, which included a couple of his best mates, were being sent to Hong Kong, a British Colony and military base since 1856. There followed a few more months of training and preparation before leaving in December 1938 when they sailed to Hong Kong on the troop ship Lancashire anchored in Liverpool which took them via Gibraltar, Port Said in Egypt, Aden, Bombay, Ceylon and Singapore. To a teenager, this must have seemed like a tour of the whole world visiting amazing ports along the way, and Tom was excited to be starting his naval life at last. The voyage was mainly spent either in his bunk, or at work, and for six weeks and five days his life consisted of hard work in the hot and steamy engine room but also a lot of joking and fun with his fellow sailors.

Hong Kong was hot and humid and Tom was glad of his "Number 6" lightweight, white tropical issue uniform supplied for overseas use. He and his contingent were registered at HMS

Tamar which was a shore base on Hong Kong, very similar in some respects to the barracks he had known at Drake in Plymouth. The same imposing gates at the entrance to the large colonial building, the base was named after the fifth HMS Tamar ship built in 1863, an iron screw troop ship which became a base ship in Hong Kong in 1897 and was to be scuttled in 1941. The ship was moored alongside the Naval base and was used as part of the main buildings.

Hong Kong had been a British Colony since 1847 when the Manchu Dynasty in China had suffered defeat, and it formed an important military and trading base in the East. By the 1890's Hong Kong was ultra-modern, with electric lighting and a good tram system. In the 1920's the British Governor, his colonial secretary and anyone in authority lived in luxury on The Peak, the cool heights above the capital city Victoria.

Major changes were to begin in the 1940's and 1950's when a large proportion of Chinese migrants would arrive from mainland China fleeing war and by then 90% of the total population of Hong Kong was Chinese. But in the years before World War Two it was a pleasant region with green hillsides and mainly single storey colonial buildings. Many of the shops were run by Chinese workers and there were clubs, restaurants and a well attended horse racing circuit named Happy Valley Racecourse.

Happy Valley was built in 1845 to provide horse racing for the British living in Hong Kong. The area used for the racecourse had been swamp land, but was the only suitable flat area for racing on the island. To make way for the racecourse the Hong Kong government banned the local people from growing rice, drained the area and the first race was run in 1846. Racing quickly became a favourite pastime among the Chinese population too.

In 1918 one of the grandstands had collapsed, knocking over

hot food stalls which set bamboo matting on fire. About five hundred people tragically died in the blaze.

Hunting parties were arranged to hunt the indigenous civet cat, and the ladies whiled away the hours playing bridge, attending parties, balls and bazaars. Life was easy and enjoyable, and yet the Chinese resented being under British rule. In 1925 a revolt by the Chinese workers led to 100,000 of them leaving the colony and many menial tasks had to be done by the British. Trade suffered badly too.

Stepping ashore in Hong Kong in 1939 would surely have been an incredible experience for a seasoned traveller; but for Tom aged eighteen, a newly fledged sailor it was to be the most wonderful, confusing, amazing place in the world! The six week voyage from Plymouth had been full time, strenuous work in the engine rooms, but he had had time to relax too. And here he was, in his tropical whites in the heat and humidity of South West China, walking down the gangplank starting his new life. The newly arrived naval ratings settled in and were given leave to explore the colony.

British influence had been uppermost in the architecture there, and large department stores and British clubs were plentiful. Sunday was religiously observed and special days such as the Monarch's birthday and St George's Day were celebrated. New textile businesses had been established and were exporting goods which undercut prices in Britain. The owners of these became rich and set up their own Chamber of Commerce, built large houses in Gothic style and opened clubs for the Chinese workers to join. The workers lived mainly in tenements in the Kowloon area, but the Victorian European style of building along the waterfront gave it a mediterranean look.

And so Tom began his career dividing his time between the base at HMS Tamar and week-long sailings on HMS Thracian to patrol the waters of the South China Sea looking for enemy ships and then practicing laying mines in Hong Kong Harbour to stall any impending attack (rumours of which could not be ignored).

Japanese troops were advancing in Manchuria fighting the Chinese there and, although this was a long way from Hong Kong, trouble was edging closer. Shanghai had fallen in 1937 and then Nanking with the appalling massacre of three hundred thousand Chinese civilians and the rape of up to fifty thousand Chinese women. Japan was then turning its attention to South China, capturing main ports along the coast. Hong Kong became an all-important centre for co-ordination of supplies to the port, as China's Chiang Kai-Shek and his government retreated to the Sichuan province.

HMS Thracian had been launched in 1920 at Newcastle and then towed to HM Dockyard at Sheerness where the build was completed in 1922. Its motto was "Thrust On" and in 1939 she was deployed with Hong Kong local flotilla for patrol duties in the China Sea. Converted to a mine-layer she was capable of carrying forty mines and laid a defensive minefield in the Lantau Channel, and a further field at Shap, Hong Kong. During patrols in 1940 and 1941 Thracian laid a further one hundred and forty mines at West Lamma.

New industrial units were being built in Hong Kong by industrialists from Shanghai who withdrew to the colony away from Japanese control. Japan could see that capturing the colony would be a prize worth having and with Britain in the grip of war with Germany it seemed their chance had come.

There was a buzz which caught up the British sailors in Hong Kong in the noisy main streets from which narrow side streets climbed up each side full of Chinese traders selling carved jade or ivory, flowers, cooked food and live birds in cages. Each evening Tom and his mates were allowed shore leave and joined in with the noisy nightlife whenever they could – eating out, dancing at the dance halls and during daytime leave either heading for the seashore – a favourite one being the Big Wave Beach – swimming, or taking in the scenery from the cooler high points which were reached on a cable car.

Thirteen

*Major General Christopher Michael Maltby was Commander of
the Hong Kong Garrison commanding a force of ten thousand men*

Slowly at first, the streets and the evening scenes changed. With worries about the British civilians being caught up in the war if Japan did capture Hong Kong, the women and children of service personnel were shipped out and taken to Australia in 1940. The husbands left behind were not pleased about this evacuation especially as the threat from the Japanese had recently gone quiet. However there was much for them to do. The colony was now being increased in size by the huge influx of Chinese escaping the war on the mainland. They set up factories and more shops where it was assumed a safe haven for them to work and live.

In the Roman Calendar, the fifteenth of March was known as 'The Ides of March' as it was chosen to observe some of their religious beliefs, and it also marked the first full moon of their new year. It became a notorious date when Julius Caesar was stabbed to death, having been warned by a seer that he would die before the Ides of March. Shakespeare dramatised this meeting between the soothsayer and Caesar when he tells him "Beware the Ides of March!".

The fifteenth of March 1941 was an auspicious day for Tom too – he became twenty one years old. His 'coming of age' began for him working in his role as Leading Stoker deep in the engine room of HMS Thracian preparing her for patrol operations, but that evening Tom and some of his mates were given shore leave until 11pm. They would head for the popular hotel bar where they could buy drinks, cigarettes and listen to the music. Even in this uncertain time for Hong Kong life continued almost as normal and people danced and sang. Tom recalled the birthdays of his childhood and how happy everyone was to sing to him.

Then the terrible news arrived on 7 December 1941 that the Japanese had bombed Pearl Harbour, Hawaii, and damaged much of the American fleet there. Nearly two thousand, five hundred American servicemen were killed and one thousand, one hundred and seventy eight wounded. All eight US battleships were damaged but six of these were returned to service following repairs. Other vessels were sunk or damaged too, plus nearly two hundred aircraft.

The Japanese lost twenty nine planes, five mini-submarines and sixty four servicemen. Tom was working on HMS Thracian when he heard the news about Pearl Harbour. He felt proud to be employed making the waters around Hong Kong safe against a possible attack by the Japanese.

The surprise attack at Pearl Harbour led to the United States entering the war. The Japanese were gaining in strength and power and there were permanent look-outs now on the hills above Hong Kong fearing an attack from the Japanese via the mainland of China. Hong Kong was now very vulnerable to invasion by the Japanese. Two battalions of Canadian troops were brought in to increase the manpower should there be an attack.

Major General Maltby realised that the task of defending the island would be difficult if not impossible and he used the next three months to upgrade the defences he had in order to hold Hong Kong and deny the harbour access to the Japanese.

He formed a mainland Brigade out of three battalions; the

Second Royal Scots; a battalion of Punjabi soldiers and also the 5/7 Rajputs. Together with support from batteries of Hong Kong and Singapore Royal Artillery plus an Indian Army Regiment who took on some locally enlisted Chinese. The defending line was set across the Kowloon Gap, locally known as the 'Gin Drinker's Line', and Hong Kong Island would be defended by the Canadian battalions whose job it was to hold the pillboxes around the island perimeter. Gin Drinkers Line (named after the Gin Drinker's Bay in Kwai Chung) had been constructed in 1936–1938 on the same defensive idea as the Maginot Line had been in France. It fronted the mountains of the Kowloon Peninsula and prevented any southward invasion from the New Territories in the North. It had a series of defence posts linked by paths. Bunkers, trenches and artillery batteries were installed along its fifteen mile length.

Their fears were realised in early December, the very day of the attack on Pearl Harbour, when there was the sound of bomber aircraft filling the skies overhead as thirty six Japanese attack planes bombed Kai Tak Airfield destroying RAF bombers and flying boats plus some civilian aircraft. The runway was very badly damaged too. Meanwhile Japanese troops advanced across the Sham Chun River and there was heavy fighting by both sides as the Japanese invaded Hong Kong, as expected from the northern mainland.

The British garrisons were spurred into action, fixing bayonets on rifles and advancing towards the Japanese who had crept towards them under cover of darkness during the bombing raid. The Japanese continued their advance and overran the poorly manned Gin Drinker's Line often at night, causing the allied troops to abandon Kowloon, scuttling vessels as they retreated.

Hand to hand fighting took place in several areas on the main island, but with heavy casualties General Maltby finally conceded defeat on Christmas Day, after six days of piecemeal conflict. He gave the order to evacuate all personnel back to Hong Kong Island. He also ordered that all the gold bullion stored in the banks of Hong Kong was to be sent off by ship which meant that both HMS Tenidous and HMS Scout being used, leaving just HMS Thracian to defend the harbour.

The battle for Hong Kong lasted until 24th December 1941, during which time many troops and civilians were either killed while fighting, or experienced the atrocious behaviour of the Japanese. A field hospital treating British soldiers was destroyed, the patients and nursing staff savagely murdered.

The Japanese then called for the British to surrender but this was refused. The Royal Navy launched a flotilla of motor boats into the harbour to try to prevent the Japanese infantry crossing the water towards the island. This did not go well with many British casualties and troops being killed or captured by the Japanese. In all one thousand five hundred and fifty men died in the attempt to defend the colony.

General Maltby ordered the formal surrender of Hong Kong after losing many personnel and with many more injured, but was praised by Winston Churchill for having put up such brave resistance depleting Japanese numbers, aircraft and shipping. It was Christmas Day 1941.

Japanese General Chijo Takashi Sakai took the surrender.

Fourteen

*In times of crisis, the engine-room floor became
a place of refuge where a little sleep could be
had before the next hours of work.*

Tom and the crew of HMS Thracian were in dock waiting to
have an extra gun mounted on the aft of the ship when they
heard about the attack and ultimate surrender to the Japanese.
Fitting the gun was abandoned and all haste was made to
evacuate troops who had been cut off from their bases. During
this evacuation, the ship ran aground on rocks at night. With
some clever manoeuvring the ship was freed to carry on her
mission but the bottom of two oil storage tanks were ripped out
and a boiler was out of action.

Thracian managed to carry out not only rescue missions, but
was able to sink, or scuttle as it was known, fourteen merchant
ships in the harbour to prevent them being taken by the enemy.
A congratulatory signal was received by the Thracian from the
Royal Naval Command for the courageous work done by this
lone ship.

Tom and his mates in the engine room were proud of the
honour but were now exhausted and took turns sleeping on the
floor whilst heading for the dockyard to get the ship repaired.
This was found to be impossible as the Japanese had set up
artillery ranges over the front of Hong Kong and no shipping
could get near the docks. It was decided they should make for

the dry dock at Aberdeen which could be reached away from the artillery range. Bad news there too – all the dockyard workers had deserted in fear of their lives, so the Thracian docked as best she could, but was besieged by bad luck, getting damaged when bombs fell nearby. Fire in the engine room meant they had to shut down the boilers, but they were able to help by giving first aid to injured servicemen on the dockside.

The final sailing was made over to Repulse Bay where HMS Thracian was beached and the crew were taken to the Aberdeen shore base. For the next few days sailors became soldiers, joining the Canadian troops on the Peak, dodging rifle fire from the enemy and hiding in the wooded hillsides.

Soon, however, the Canadians and Royal Navy were rounded up and taken prisoner, some to a nearby convent, others to the North Point prison camp.

Britain and Japan had been allies from 1902 until 1921. Indeed in World War One Japan sent ships to the Mediterranean to protect British convoys.

Japan defeated Russia in the 1905 Russo-Japanese War, and by the Treaty of Portsmouth acquired the rights to Manchuria, a region of China formerly owned by Russia on a lease issued in 1898. The Washington conference in 1921 established peace in the Far East and a pact was made that power would be shared in the ratio 3:5:5 between Japan, Britain and the USA.

It was an uneasy peace, and Japan withdrew from the League of Nations in 1932 after the Lytton Commission declared the Japanese take-over of Manchuria to be illegal. 1935 saw Japan walk out of the London Naval Conference when parity of their navy with the United States was refused. By 1937 Japan started undeclared war with china, which escalated when Chiang Kai-Shek refused to settle peacefully on Japan's terms.

The United States wanted Japan to make peace with China

but they refused, making small inroads into the vast country. The war in Europe began and in 1940 Japan signed a pact with Germany and Italy and thus became a real threat to Hong Kong and the Far East.

Fifteen

Taken prisoner, the men were forced to carry heavy equipment and supplies to their destined internment camp.

On 29th December 1941 Tom was marching, but slowly, more of an amble really. Weighed down by a kitbag slung on his back, and sporting a hefty bruise on the side of his face – his captors had shown him little mercy when he had been captured and used a heavy stick to deliver punishment – he had joined the ranks of a column of prisoners of war and was also carrying a heavy camp cooker salvaged from their base. He was just one of about four hundred men, both army and navy, being marched to the prisoner of war camp at North Point. Several of his comrades fell by the wayside on this march, unable to walk any further due to illness or brutal treatment from their captors who carried, and often used, heavy wooden sticks or rifle butts to punish 'weak' prisoners who faltered and fell.

Tom's group diminished to about two thirds of those who set out and, after a gruelling uphill section, they reached North Point Camp. Put to work right away, it was necessary to dispose of dead Japanese soldiers, Chinese civilians and horses along the sea front where they had fallen during the invasion. It would have been a terrible sight, with men, women and children's bodies floating in the sea alongside the camp. Bloated, stinking corpses were buried or burned and the best was made of the filthy living quarters which had been looted and stripped bare by the local

Chinese people. Those found not to be 'pulling their weight' were given a hefty whack by a Japanese guard wielding a stick.

Prisoners had to bow to every Japanese guard or officer, regardless of their rank, and regardless too of the inhumane treatment regularly used on their pals.

There was no escape from the relentless beatings, kickings, beheadings and trial by torture which happened daily. The men not only had to deal with the heavy workload and little food but had to be strong enough to carry the shame they felt when they could not help or save a fellow comrade's life.

Another punishment favoured by the guards was to make a man stand in the hot sun or pouring rain for several hours holding a bucket of sand above their head with their arms straight. The guards would watch for any sign of lowering of the bucket, ready to dish out more brutal hitting with the heavy stick. Men would be further punished by being buried up to their neck and left in the hot sun all day. Some had fingernails pulled out or teeth extracted brutally. If a man could not take his punishment and fell without standing up again he would be kicked until he stood. Tall men were particularly disliked by the Japanese and were made to bend down to receive their punishment.

Hundreds more prisoners of war arrived next day and confused orders were shouted as groups of men were herded into further 'marching parties' to be interned elsewhere.

Gone was the stifling heat and humidity of the Hong Kong Tom had known, replaced by storms, rain and high winds which caused huge waves to crash in and swamp the huts nearest to the shore. The men were put to work on burial duties, burying the many Japanese, Chinese and British who had fallen during the invasion by the Japanese forces. This was heavy work which had to be done with little food to keep them going. Those not on burial duty were ordered to dismantle heavy machinery and any armament placements which were damaged but of use to the Japanese in their own country. This scrap metal had to be carried to the harbour and loaded onto merchant ships heading for Japan.

There was little food so that hunger was always gnawing at their stomachs, and the poor weather took its toll on the prisoners who succumbed to diseases such as dysentery, malaria, pellagra, scurvy, pneumonia and beriberi. Many died as a result of these distressing diseases.

All these diseases were debilitating and were mainly caused by a poor diet, excessive labour in extreme heat and tropical rain. The diet was so meagre and was usually a small bowl of rice with a watery vegetable soup. The rice was polished white rice and the health-giving brown covering on each grain had been removed. The Japanese knew they had to take extra thiamine – vitamin B1 – to compensate for this as their diet was rice-based anyway. But food given to prisoners was rarely, if ever, supplemented with the vitamin. This led to the disease beriberi, either wet or dry. The symptoms of wet beriberi were sudden and extreme, the lack of thiamine causing heart and circulation problems. 'Electric Feet' or 'Happy Feet' was a symptom and would drive men to distraction as their feet felt as if they were being burned. Men would swell up with oedema, fluid retention, their arms, legs and torso filled with extra fluid and the most distressing effect was the way the scrotum swelled – often to the size of a grapefruit. The neck, throat and lungs became full of fluid and men died choking and making the noise of a croaking frog. This was known to the prisoners as the 'beriberi song'.

Dry beriberi caused tremendous pain and damage to the nervous system and muscles. Leg cramps, numb toes making walking difficult and eventually the man suffered with 'foot-drop' where the foot hangs limp in a straight line down from the lower leg.

Other diseases were rife. Scurvy due to lack of vitamin C and Pellagra caused by a lack of the vitamin Niacin or B3 where a man's skin looks sunburned and starts to peel and bleed. Fungal infections were often present in the hot wet conditions and many prisoners suffered from dysentery – an inflammatory disease of the intestine causing severe diarrhoea and pain.

Any small cut or lesion on the ankle or leg could quickly turn into a tropical ulcer which became infected, often exposing the bone beneath the skin. The infected material gathering in the ulcer would need to be cleaned out and the medics did what they could for these sufferers by scooping out the detritus with a sharpened spoon, or placing maggots in the ulcer to eat the contents. A number of amputations were necessary where the ulcer would not heal and these had to be carried out quickly with no anaesthetic, the prisoner held down while the surgeon removed the leg.

The men also had worries about their relatives at home during the war that was raging there, and how long the conflict would last. They had little or no news from the home front, and the stories they heard made them wonder at their validity. The local Chinese civilians who lived near the prisoner of war camps still ran shops and would hawk supplies to the camps when they could. They would bring cigarettes and some food to sell to the prisoners across the wire fences when the guards were not looking. The prisoners did have some money as they would be paid a small wage for the work they carried out in camp.

Smoking was considered normal. Both the Japanese guards and officers and the prisoners would smoke when cigarettes were available. Smoking was in fact authorised under the Geneva Convention and should be made available to prisoners. The Japanese preferred their own brand of cigarettes which were short, stubby ones filled with rough-cut strong tobacco. When there was a lack of supplies, men would roll up whatever local 'baccy' they could get their hands on and the Chinese would often trade across the wire perimeter fence and provide a tobacco which came to be known as 'Wog' or 'Granny's Armpit' such was the unusual odour it produced from the long strands of tobacco. Cigarette papers were rarely found either and the pages of bibles were often torn out to use.

Sixteen

With little or no news from the outside, the prisoners of war could only hope for rescue from their awful treatment in the camp.

Three months had passed and in April Tom and about two hundred others were rounded up and marched to another camp called Sham Shui Po, a former British Army Barracks. This camp was further around the coast and proved to be freezing cold, stark, bare barracks with nothing but walls, concrete floors and a bit of roofing in places. This camp held about two thousand prisoners of war, British Army, Hong Kong Volunteer Defence Corps, Royal Naval Dockyard Police and Royal Navy. Once again the barracks had been stripped of all contents and the men had to find what they could in order to make it habitable again.

To begin with there was food. Rice and tinned meat or a small piece of fish and some vegetables. The tinned meat was corned beef, known to the men as 'bully beef' which got its nickname from the French 'boeuf bouilli' or boiled beef. The canning of this salted beef was a popular method of preserving and distributing beef to troops overseas but was also widely used in the home during wartime rationing. The beef was treated and cooked with rock salt (or 'corns' of salt – corns meaning hard grains). Thus the name corned beef was adopted by the manufacturers in South America where the beef was processed. This food gradually ran out in the camp and then only rice was boiled to eat. Here, again, poor diet and hygiene could only result in men dying of disease and hunger.

There were numerous 'burial' duties and latrine digging groups but apart from that the guards found work for the prisoners to do. Continually shouted orders were given to move heavy beams of metal across an open area or repairing the accommodation for hours on end. The men could not rest even when in a state of near collapse. The camp kept to Tokyo time, rather than the local Chinese time, which meant that early parade each day was at 5am, summer and winter.

A special working party of five hundred prisoners was selected to work on repairing and extending the airport at Kai Tak. This working party would be marched out of the camp at 4am to make the journey on foot of three miles ready to begin their twelve hour day of heavy labour. They had to dig with poor quality shovels and move the soil and stones in wheelbarrows to tip away at the runway sides. There was no rest during the day and then the three mile march back to camp in the evening. Even sick men were commandeered to join this work party, so desperate were the Japanese to get the runway ready for their own use.

Letters were written and somehow smuggled out by bribing local Chinese people who were always to be found at the prison camp border wire. The Chinese were taking a big risk in being seen near the border wire, if caught they were tortured and killed by the Japanese guards. Red Cross parcels were commandeered by the Japanese so rarely if ever got shared out to the prisoners. Small keepsakes were carved from bamboo, chess sets were made and even dentures were fashioned from bits of wood and teeth taken from dead bodies they were ordered to bury – eagerly and gratefully used by prisoners who had lost their teeth through disease.

Tom and a few comrades turned a patch of ground into a sort

of garden where seeds and fruit pips were grown into something 'edible'. Tom became expert at fly swatting and the game was to see how many you could kill with one swat!

An electric fence surrounded the camp and this was used by the Japanese to torture the Chinese locals who would stand near the fence trying to sell or trade things with the prisoners. Both men and women, if caught, were bound together with wire, drenched with water and the end of the wire would be thrown over the electric fence causing them all to scream in agony – much to the amusement of the Japanese guards. Often a guard would order a prisoner to kneel in the dirt and he would draw his sword just to see the look of terror on the man's face. With beheadings randomly carried out, the men never knew whether their time had actually come or if it was just the guard's idea of amusement.

Despite the inhumane conditions and punishments, the prisoners of war had their own fun where possible, telling jokes and putting on impromptu plays kept their minds active and relieved the stress of everyday hardship. An old mess tin and a piece of bamboo served as a drum, and one or two men were good at fashioning flutes from a length of bamboo in which they cut holes along the side. A concert would be put on to entertain not only themselves, but their Japanese guards would also enjoy watching, whether they understood the words and songs or not! Loud applause would ring out at the end.

Some would be good at drawing and those who were very good were able to swap a sketch for an extra piece of food. Some of these sketches survived the war and proved to be accurate records of the conditions at the time.

Red Cross parcels were received at the camps, but were kept by the guards and so it was quite ironic that a sketch could be swapped for a tin of good old corned beef. The only items in the parcels the Japanese threw away, not knowing what on earth it could be, were jars of Marmite. The men would retrieve these from the rubbish bins and eagerly incorporate it into their diet providing themselves with a vital source of vitamin B.

Prisoners existed somehow on the very poor diet of rice and watery vegetable soup leading to severe malnutrition, exhaustion and making them susceptible to disease. The rice sometimes had weevils and insects in it and the men joked that it gave them some protein. Their low resistance to malaria and tropical ulcers added to their health problems. The supply of drugs and medical equipment was almost non-existent and death was commonplace.

Keepsakes were fashioned from bits of wood to be hidden away to take home after the war. Chess pieces, dice, draughts and counters were made out of pieces of scrap wood found lying around.

One day at morning roll-call the Japanese guard gave each man a piece of paper which they were to sign saying they would not try to escape. A group of about ten refused to sign it and were subjected to twelve hours standing in the parade ground in torrential tropical rain, and being threatened by a firing squad, before they agreed to sign.

After two months of surviving each day and wondering what the future held for them, the prisoners began to hear rumours that they were to be sent to Japan. Surely anything would be better than this existence with the starvation, disease and beatings they endured.

In July 1942 Tom's eldest sister (his next of kin) received a letter to say that he was a prisoner of war and that he was therefore alive, not just listed as 'missing'.

Diphtheria was rife at Sham Shui Po and five or six men a day were dying from this fast moving very contagious disease. The guards probably decided this disease was endangering them also and in early September all prisoners were ordered onto the parade ground. On the twenty fifth of September 1942, one thousand, eight hundred and sixteen prisoners of war were marched out of the camp towards the coast.

Seventeen

The harbour near Sham Shui Po was called Bamboo Harbour and it was from this dockside that small boats could ferry men and supplies out to the large waiting ships.

Spirits were a little higher among the prisoners as they were counted, numbered, photographed and vaccinated. New boots and kit were issued and extra food was given out. Next morning at 5.30am after roll-call they were marched under the orders of Tsuyaki Nimori (the former camp interpreter of Sham Shui Po) to the jetty entrance to the harbour and were made to stand and wait for two hours for a Japanese General who gave a speech – shouting to the whole assembled parade – the shouting Tom was hearing brought him out of his dream and he was in that hot, stinking hold of the ship and orders were being shouted down through the hatch …

Eighteen

American submarines were patrolling the waters of
the China Sea firing at any enemy Japanese shipping.
USS Grouper was such a submarine, three hundred
feet long and armed with twenty-four torpedoes.

It seems as if the ship is about to set sail and with the light from the open hatch Tom can make out the makeshift plank flooring barely covering a cargo of metal sheets and machinery destined for Osaka, Japan, and many ballast sacks of sand. Hidden from view are about thirty tons of explosives in the form of shells being transported to Tokyo. History would label this freighter as one of the 'hell ships' but the captive, suffering men already know what hell it is.

It is possible only to sit cross legged and there is no room to lie down. When the allotted number are in the hold the hatches are shut and it is dark as night, with just one small light on the inside of the hatch cover. Tom tries to take a deep breath of the hot rancid air but it does little to soothe his lungs.

The air soon becomes fetid and stale again, there is little water he is thirsty; toilet facilities, when the men are not allowed up on deck to use the latrines, consist of buckets on ropes let down into the hold which are then hauled up again and emptied. The men suffer from diarrhoea, dysentery beri beri, pellagra and other diseases. With no time now to arrange latrine parties and, demeaning as it is, the bottom of the hold becomes its own stinking latrine adding to the bad air around them. Falling asleep probably save many of the men's lives as in sleep their heart rate and metabolism slow down thus preventing the worst ravages of heatstroke.

'Oh, for some movement of the ship' – so that at least they could hope for better air and regain a little dignity again. The night brings some relief from the heat and by morning it is cool and a breakfast of bread and tea and some cigarettes was lowered down for the prisoners. After a second day of waiting there is a very noisy battalion of Japanese soldiers coming on board and they occupy the upper parts of the hold. They are laughing and talking loudly, obviously excited about going home. This seems to be the signal for the ship to set sail and early next morning, the twenty seventh of September, it departs. All prisoners are allowed on deck for an hour as they leave Hong Kong. They sailed at 8am, steaming past Stanley Point which re-awakened memories of the battle they had fought there, but as they made for the open sea the prisoners were again ordered down below.

The ship at last begins to move and roll about on the South China Sea and then the East China Sea as they make their way along the coast of China and on to Japan. The movement causes fresh problems; some men are seasick adding to the stinking 'bilge' at the bottom of the hold which now slops from side to side with the ship's rolling. Tom's thoughts are frequently of home now and the familiar movement of the ship is his only comfort. Many of his comrades are sick and thirsty, but a few still manage to joke about their appalling conditions. Alf is also now in Hold One and is recalling events from the night Hong Kong fell to the Japanese and his terrible ordeal being injured and in the water but eventually being rescued. His stories are eagerly listened to by them all.

Jokes are told too, prayers are muttered, a few of the men even try singing in the hope their spirits would rise a little – anything to keep up morale. One soldier in number two hold had managed to bring his piano accordion on board and plays songs they are all able to join in with. There is roll call each morning at 6am and each evening at 6pm on deck. There is a new supply of food – better than they have had for some time, with bully beef, rice and bread. There is even a supply of cigarettes. There is no water for washing only one tap on deck where they are able to fill water bottles twice a day.

Sleeping is difficult on the lumpy sandbags which are becoming very wet and smelly and the only way to use the latrines lashed to the side of the ship is by clambering over sleepy bodies lying on these sandbags, and climbing several ladders to the upper deck where there is a constant queue for the latrine. Conditions worsen every day, and now diphtheria takes a hold on many of the prisoners. The worst cases are put on deck on blankets. This they endure for three days – each day seeming to last as long as a week.

Nineteen

'Maru' – all Japanese merchant ships are given the suffix Maru, the written ideographic character meaning 'round'. It is generally supposed that this custom dates back to medieval times when the Daimyo named their vessels after their castles – wherein the central part is the Hon-maru.

The Lisbon Maru was flying the Japanese flag and displayed no flag or marking to indicate that prisoners of war were on board.

A continual threat to the Japanese ships in these waters was the presence of American submarines patrolling the South China Sea on the lookout for enemy ships. One such submarine was the SS Grouper which was travelling at a speed of six knots just off the coast of China and at 4am on the first of October 1942 she picked up a target heading north. She turned to face 180 degrees from the current tracking and waited silently for the approaching Japanese merchant ship. The ship was the Lisbon Maru.

After many men had been taken ashore due to disease, or death, the number of prisoners now amounted to one thousand eight hundred and sixteen. Also aboard the Lisbon Maru were two thousand Japanese soldiers of Chujo Takashi Sakai's 23rd army. This shipment of soldiers and POWs was dispatched on the orders of the new Chiji (governor) of Hong Kong, Shosho Rensuke Isogai.

Just before tenko on 1 Oct the Lisbon Maru was rocked by a

loud explosion; her engines stopped, the lights went out. Sentries at each hatch were doubled. Hatches were not battened down but were covered with tarpaulins secured with ropes. Lieutenant Colonel Stewart, the senior British officer, repeatedly appealed for the hatches to be opened as the prisoners of war were suffocating, and they had run out of drinking water. In response Nimori had a bucket of urine lowered into Stewart's hold. Some men had diphtheria and began to succumb more rapidly to its effects, many fainted after being forced to pump out number three hold which was making water.

The Lisbon Maru had changed course several times when she became aware of the submarine sending out torpedoes. She had avoided three torpedoes but the fourth one hit a propeller and exploded, killing a Japanese sailor.

Twenty

*Captain Kyoda Shigeru is in command of his ship
the Lisbon Maru and is making preparations for
his return to Japan and his waiting family.*

Tom wakes to the sound of men groaning and writhing in their pain and suffering from whichever disease they are burdened with. The air is putrid, the floor awash with bodily fluids and the stench is overwhelming.

Tom suddenly had to chuckle quietly as he remembered his favourite Welsh exclamation "Ych y fi!" and, just as quickly, he fell silent again to listen to the noises on board. There are sounds of a swooshing noise too, followed by a loud boom. A dull thud jolts the side of the ship and he knows by that sound that a torpedo has struck them. The torpedo has been fired by the American submarine USS Grouper SS214 belonging to Division 81 of the US Pacific Fleet Submarine Force.

On the night of 2nd and 3rd October the Japanese troops are taken off the Lisbon Maru and moved on to a transport tow vessel while the prisoners of war remain on the crippled ship which begins to list rapidly. Lieutenant Colonel Stewart organises a small group who try to break out of the hold. Tom and a few others squeeze through a hole in the tarpaulin onto the deck and ask to speak via one colleague who spoke Japanese and could interpret. The Japanese guards open fire on the group. Lieutenant Howell, RASC, who managed to break out was among the party. He was shot and later died of his wounds. Lieutenant Potter and the interpreter manage to scramble back to Stewart reporting that the ship is sinking rapidly. The remaining men are hurriedly ushered back into their dark prison. The small light eventually went out in the hold which had now been battened down. The Japanese soldiers were shouting and screaming up on the deck, the noise only slowly subsiding as they were taken off the stricken ship onto the rescue ship bound for Japan.

A whole night was spent in the listing ship's bowels, sounds of water swilling about became louder and cracking noises were heard as the bulkhead started to break up. Then someone was at the hatchway who had a knife and started to push it between the boards and cut the tarpaulin. Suddenly there was daylight as hundreds of prisoners pushed forward and out onto the sloping deck. A few guards raised their guns, but were soon overcome. The air was merciful, the sea beckoned and men slid or jumped into the sea and swam or held onto floating debris in the water.

At the same time, a group of soldiers of the Royal Scots cut ropes and get out and release all others from all three holds. All available strength is now put to the test to climb the metal ladders, made slippery with sweat and other fluids. One of the ladders broke under the weight of the struggling men, sending many crashing down onto others waiting below. Many use the broken ladder fixings still on the ship's wall together with rivets to climb up. All who had not been suffocated or drowned already are on deck. Men are in the sea, a few managing to swim the four or five miles to a small island.

Japanese ships are not picking up those in the sea who are struggling, in fact they are deliberately mowing them down. Cruelly, as men swam away and faced being shot in the water, some turned back and climbed aboard their prison ship again.

The Japanese watched them struggle on board and then either shot them or kicked them overboard again. The Japanese were then taking aim and shooting at those in the water – almost as if using them for target practice.

Twenty-One

The Lisbon Maru was armed and carrying Japanese troops as well as prisoners of war. She bore no sign that she was a POW ship. The American submarine was fully justified in sinking her and no criticism has ever been made of her actions.

Alf Hunt slid down a rope into the water, marvelling at how cool it was. The side of the ship had barnacles on it which had badly cut and scratched his legs and the water soothed his skin.

The East China Sea is a broad continental shelf over which there are large tidal currents. Scientific measurements have been taken show that the tidal flow off Hangzhou Bay are the highest anywhere along the Chinese coast and can be as high as thirty feet or nine metres.

Alf swam against the strong currents towards some ships but as none of them seemed to be picking up survivors he swam on towards land he saw in the distance. His swim was aided by an old vegetable crate he managed to cling to and the tides turned in his favour as he swam about four miles to an island. There he found a small stream and was able to quench his thirst. Later he and others found out the stream they had so gladly found to drink came not from some spring, but from a toilet used by the locals further up the hill.

The Chinese on the Dongji Islands were welcoming to Alf and the other survivors and they fed and clothed them. A few days later a Japanese Navy ship picked them up and transported them to Whampou Docks, near Shanghai where they were quickly transferred onto the Shinsei Maru and taken to Moji in Japan.

Those prisoners that are picked up from the sea are taken on a Japanese ship bound for Shanghai and are mustered in Shanghai next day for tenko. Nine hundred and seventy men respond to their names, eight hundred and forty fail to answer. Six had escaped with the help of the Chinese. The survivors are put aboard the Shinsei Maru for onward transport to Japan, they are starved, beaten and abused, their guards being goaded to extremes by Captain Nimori.

Twenty-Two

The Lisbon Maru was listing badly and sinking gradually, the stern of the ship was underwater, the bow high in the air.

Tom had made an incredible effort to get out of the ship's hold for the second time, up the slippery, broken ladder and through the gap in the hatchway and slid along the tilting deck and waited by the ship's rail, deciding what was the best action to take. He took in large breaths of the fresh air but his head was buzzing with unanswered questions that this seemingly endless incarceration had stirred up in him. He had time to reflect, to wonder what was happening in the wider world and not just there on that doomed sinking ship. Tom closed his eyes against the scene in front of him.

In fact the war was indeed still raging and had intensified now that the United States was fully engaged in what had become a world war. Its car makers and other manufacturers had changed their production lines to produce weapons of war. Japanese people living in the United States were detained in internment camps and American troops gained major offensives at Midway and Coral Sea. Her air force began air raids over Japan hitting Tokyo in retaliation for Pearl Harbour. A large scale attack was being planned against Ceylon.

Intelligence was vital in times of war and cryptology could be used to protect messages and signals between control rooms and troops. These encrypted codes could be broken however and code breaking was already established in both Britain at Bletchley Park and in Hong Kong where the Government Code and Cypher School had been founded in 1935 to consolidate its work with the Far East Combined Bureau. The code breaking work pioneered at Bletchley Park had focussed on solving German coding under the leadership of Alan Turing, famous worldwide for cracking the Enigma code. Now it became necessary to de-code Japanese messages and a group of twenty undergraduates from Oxford and Cambridge Universities were given intensive training in the Japanese language and worked at Bletchley Park deciphering Japanese codes. The government, under Winston Churchill, were kept up to date with the latest deciphered messages and shared vital information with the allied troops and navies.

If Tom could open a newspaper he would have read an amazing account of the battles going on around the globe. The Battle of Stalingrad is in progress with German forces fighting the Russians. Australian and American troops have defeated the Japanese at Milne Bay, Papua, making it the first major defeat for the Japanese land forces in the Pacific War and easing the threat to Australia.

In Europe, the RAF bombed Dusseldorf with a large explosive and incendiary attack causing devastation, followed by air raids on Munich and Saarbrucken.

Nearer to Tom, Japanese air attacks had sunk some major British ships with the Repulse, Prince of Wales and Hermes being among those lost with many casualties, halting the shipping operations between Burma and India. The Japanese air campaign had been ordered by Admiral Yamamoto in his quest to destroy the British fleet.

If Tom could have read about his home town in South Wales, he would have heard about the Three Night Raid on Swansea City over the nights of the nineteenth, twentieth and twenty-first of February 1941 when German planes had dropped explosive bombs and incendiaries on the city centre causing extensive damage and lighting up the night sky for miles as the city burned. Entire streets of residential homes were gone and the main shopping centre of Swansea obliterated. Some of these bombs fell on the coastal areas as, by a full moon, the enemy planes made their noisy approach across the Loughor River, across Loughor, Kingsbridge and then on to Swansea itself.

Tom's small beach and the long bridge were not damaged.

Tom was suddenly startled and jolted awake as the ship lurched a bit further to one side and he slid over the rail and into the sea. He saw Alf and many others swimming or just floating ahead of him amongst pieces of broken wood but there were also shocking sights as bodies floated face-down in the waves. Tom began to swim and struck out as best as he could – he knew he had to put some distance between himself and the sinking vessel as a ship going down would suck the surrounding swimmers with it. He had no life jacket – these were few and far between and there were only enough for one between two men.

Weakness overcame his arms and legs, which flailed unhelpfully against the waves. Shots were being fired from the deck of the ship and bullets splashed in the water all around him. There was no chance for him in those October Tides.

Tom's life was short, yet complete. His love of the sea had beckoned him to join it and the sea enfolds him still.

The Plymouth Memorial on Plymouth Hoe lists those service personnel lost in both World War One and World War Two. Tom's name is there – it is his memorial which overlooks the Plymouth Sound – where Sir Francis Drake stood surveying the same view.

Did Tom's childhood, spent in the difficult years of the

Depression somehow prepare him for the abject humiliation and starvation in the Far East? In some small way perhaps. But there had been love and tenderness in those early years of scrimping and saving, innocence and happiness. His captors had shown him only hatred and ridicule.

Summary

Hellship losses were only two out of fifty four ships; The Montevideo Maru and the Lisbon Maru.

Most deaths by friendly fire were from submarine attacks.

Eight hundred and twenty eight men died either directly or indirectly from the sinking of the Lisbon Maru. Of the men who had tried to get into the water, eighty four went down with the ship. One thousand and six men survived and were taken into captivity in Japan where many died at the hands of their captors. Seven hundred and sixty one were eventually repatriated to the United Kingdom in August 1945.

The wreck of the Lisbon Maru lies six miles from Tung Fusham Island, off the coast of China: 29*57'N, 122*56'N.

Japan occupied Hong Kong from 1941 to 1945 when Japan surrendered at the end of World War Two.

Acknowledgements

With grateful appreciation of the wonderful COFEPOW (Children of Far East Prisoners of War) organisation for their unstinting work in keeping records of the servicemen taken prisoner in the Far East during World War 2 and for their continuing assistance given to those researching the history of their loved ones, whether they perished or returned home.

In particular, special thanks go to Pam Stubbs of the Birmingham branch of the organisation, at which she introduced me to Alf Hunt (Nobby) who assured me he remembered Tom. Thank you also to Alf's widow for allowing me to include his story and his photograph.

I am indebted to Tony Banham not only for his detailed account of the sinking of the Lisbon Maru (his book 'The Sinking of the Lisbon Maru' is published by the Hong Kong University Press), but his tireless record keeping and collecting photographs of those involved. His latest news by email to those researching relatives and interest in the ship's history is invaluable.